Measuring

Katie Dicker

Published by Evans Brothers Limited
2A Portman Mansions
Chiltern Street
London W1U 6NR

© Evans Brothers Limited 2010

Produced for Evans Brothers Limited by
White-Thomson Publishing Ltd

Printed in China by New Era Printing Co. Ltd
Printed on chlorine-free paper from sustainably managed sources.

Educational consultants: Sue Palmer MEd FRSA FEA, Dorothy Lucas MA PGCE
Project manager: Katie Dicker
Picture research: Amy Sparks
Design: Balley Design Limited
Creative director: Simon Balley
Designer/Illustrator: Andrew Li

British Library Cataloguing in Publication Data

Dicker, Katie
  Measuring. -- (Work it out)(Sparklers)
  1. Measurement--Juvenile literature.
  I. Title II. Series
  530.8-dc22

ISBN: 978 0 2375 4132 3

Contents

Measure up!

Which brother is taller?

How tall are YOU?

tip toes!

4

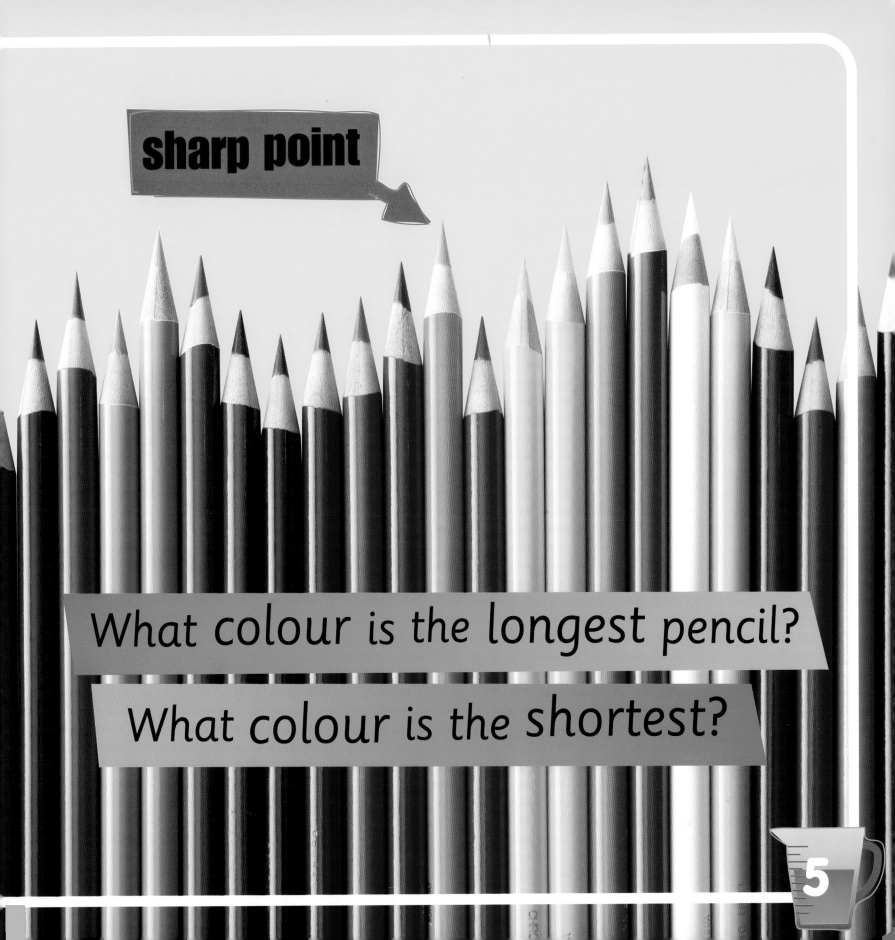

sharp point

What colour is the longest pencil?

What colour is the shortest?

5

Long line

Hang on!

Make a human chain!

How far does it stretch?

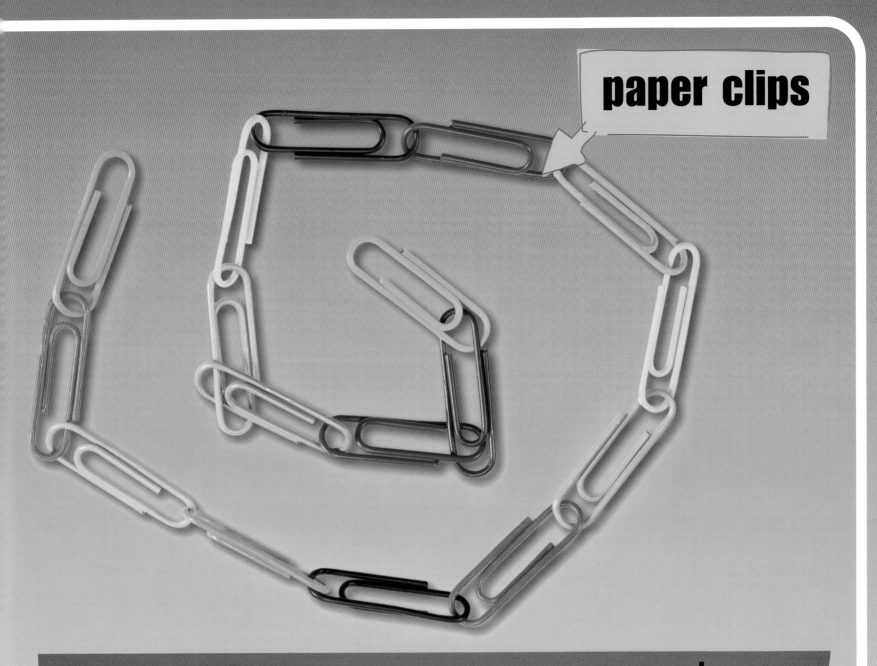

paper clips

How would you make this **line** longer or **shorter?**

Near and far

How **far** can YOU hit a ball?

Which ball is nearest to the marker?

measuring stick

9

Big and Small

finger tips

Is your hand bigger than mine?

Too big!

Where has Sam gone?

Thick and thin

Which paintbrush would YOU choose to draw the thickest line?

What's the **thinnest** piece of paper you can cut?

snip!

13

Heavy and light

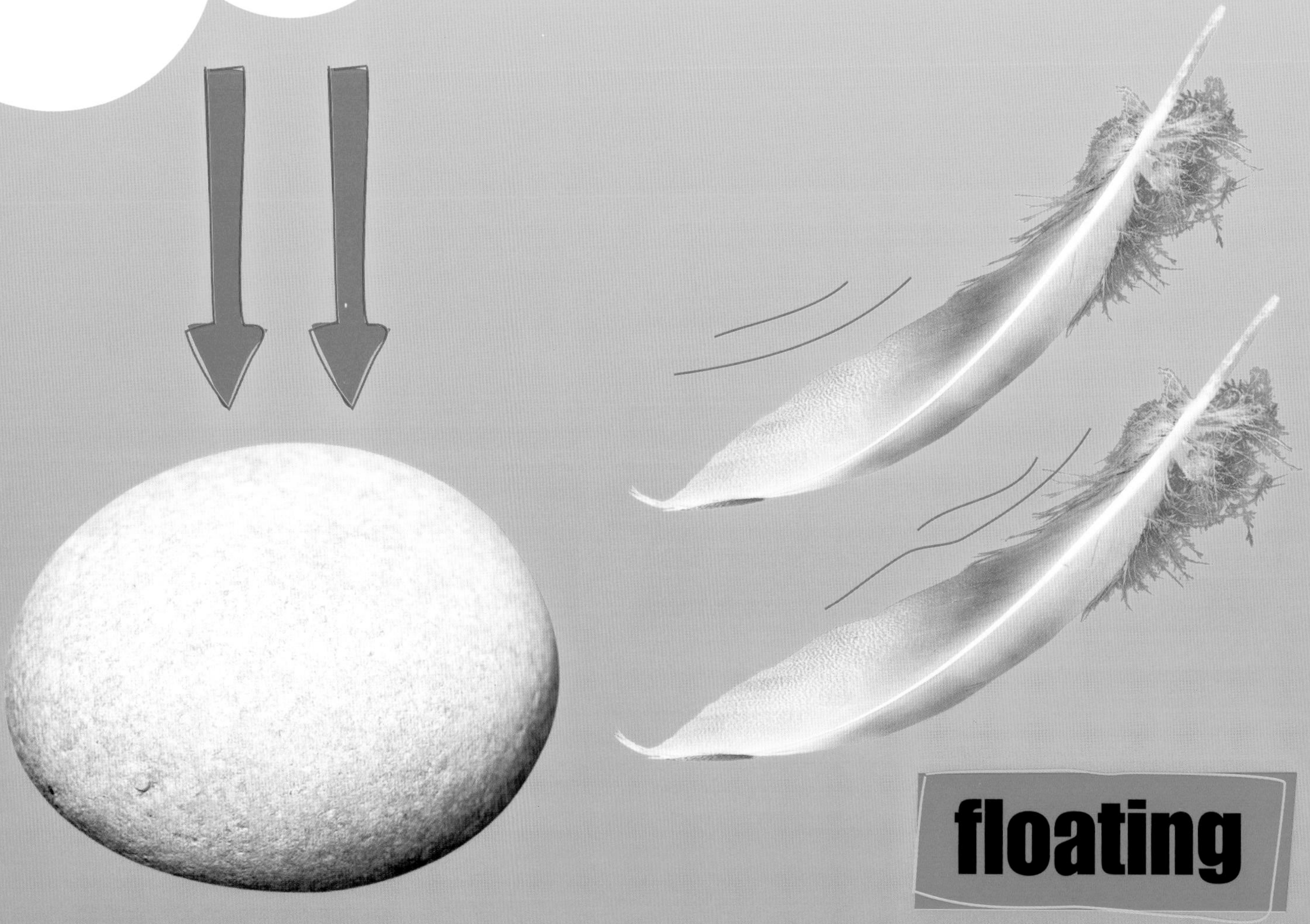

floating

Which falls faster –

the stone or the feathers?

How would YOU balance these scales?

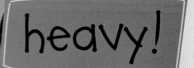

heavy!

Circus time

1,2,3,4...

How long can YOU keep a hula hoop spinning?

juggle!

How many **oranges** can this clown keep in the air?

Fill it up!

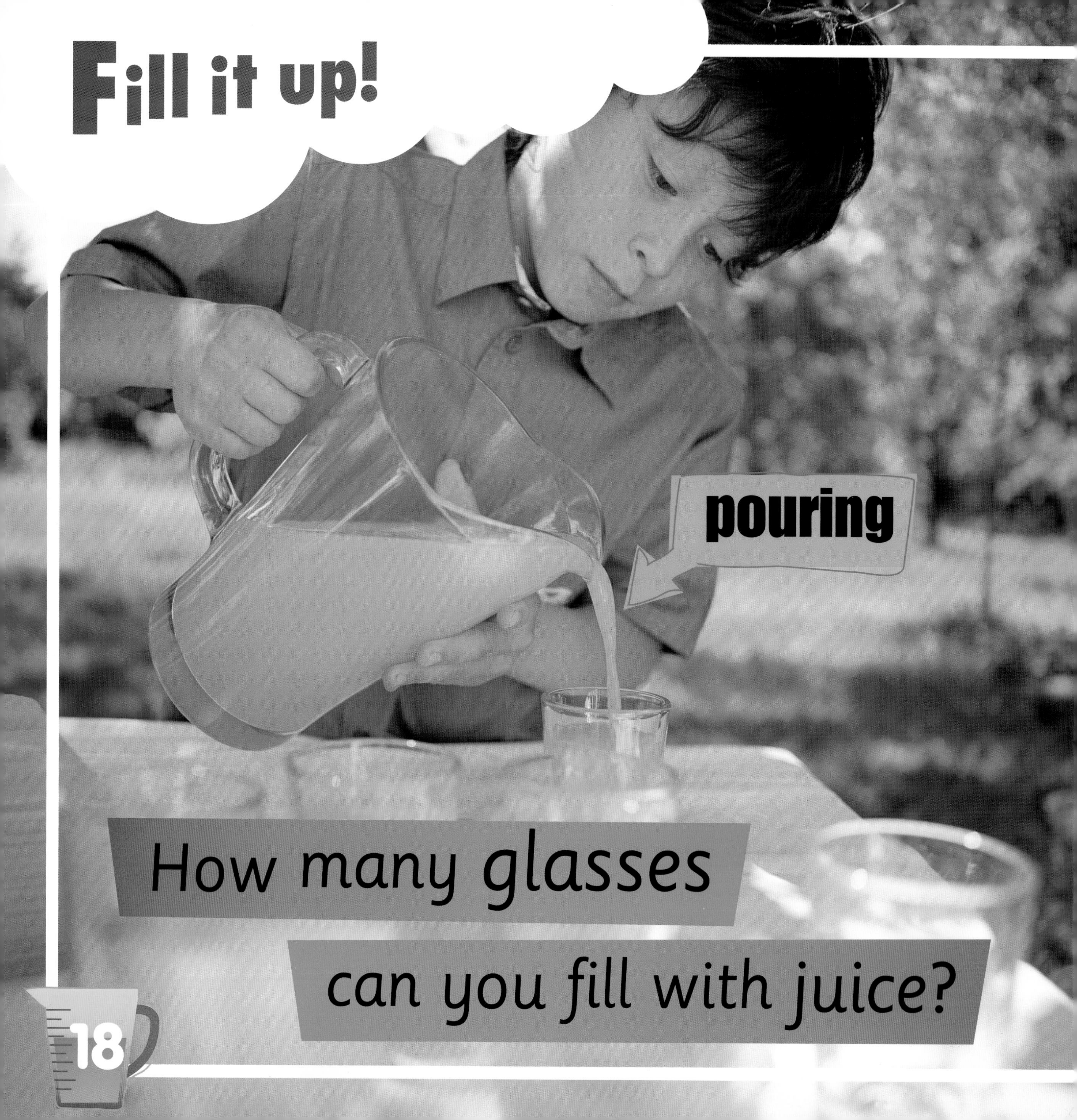

How many glasses can you fill with juice?

Which basket holds more strawberries?

juicy!

19

Hot and cold

How do YOU keep cool on a hot day?

shade

What happens to rain when it gets cold?

catch!

21

Sparklers books are designed to support and extend the learning of young children. The **Food We Eat** titles won a Practical Pre-School Silver Award, the **Body Moves** titles won a Practical Pre-School Gold Award and the **Out and About** titles won the 2009 Practical Pre-School Gold Overall Winner Award. The books' high-interest subjects link in to the Early Years curriculum and beyond. Find out more about Early Years and reading with children from the National Literacy Trust (www.literacytrust.org.uk).

Themed titles
Measuring is one of four **Work It Out** titles that encourage children to explore aspects of numeracy, reasoning and problem solving.
The other titles are:
Numbers   **Shapes**   **Solve It!**

Areas of learning
Each **Work It Out** title helps to support the following Foundation Stage areas of learning:
Personal, Social and Emotional Development
Communication, Language and Literacy
Mathematical Development
Knowledge and Understanding of the World
Physical Development
Creative Development

Making the most of reading time
When reading with younger children, take time to explore the pictures together. Ask children to find, identify, count or describe different objects. Point out colours and textures. Allow quiet spaces in your reading so that children can ask questions or repeat your words. Try pausing mid-sentence so that children can predict the next word. This sort of participation develops early reading skills.

Follow the words with your finger as you read. The main text is in Infant Sassoon, a clear, friendly font designed for children learning to read and write. The labels and sound effects add fun and give the opportunity to distinguish between levels of communication. Where appropriate, labels, sound effects or main text may be presented phonically. Encourage children to imitate the sounds.

As you read the book, you can also take the opportunity to talk about the book itself with appropriate vocabulary such as "page", "cover", "back", "front", "photograph", "label" and "page number".

You can also extend children's learning by using the books as a springboard for discussion and further activities. There are a few suggestions on the facing page.

Pages 4–5: Measure up!

Measure the heights of children over a period of time and put the markings on a wall chart to compare the rate of growth. Children may also enjoy growing their own plant seedlings to watch growth in action. Encourage children to use measuring vocabulary, such as "tall", "long" and "short" by comparing the measurements of different objects around them.

Pages 6–7: Long line

Children may enjoy making long lines by joining hands or doing the 'locomotion'. How long can they keep walking before the line breaks? Help children to make lines longer or shorter, by joining paper clips or threading beads onto a thread, for example. Discuss how 'adding' can lengthen a line, while 'taking away' can shorten it.

Pages 8–9: Near and far

Organise a series of games that have a measuring theme, such as cricket, rounders or petanque. Explain to children how hitting and throwing a ball near and far can help to win a game. Introduce the concept of time by showing that, in some games, hitting a ball a long way gives you more time to run around a course. Encourage children to keep count of the score.

Pages 10–11: Big and small

Help children to draw round their hands, feet or their whole body. You could make silhouettes by cutting the shapes from black paper. Compare the sizes in a group of children – put the largest and smallest silhouette up on the wall, or display the shapes in order of size.

Pages 12–13: Thick and thin

Encourage children to take part in a range of craft activities to hone their understanding of measurements. Ask the children to explore the effect of thick and thin paintbrushes, to cut paper into different-sized strips, and to make collages with different-sized shapes. You could also show children how to lengthen lines by joining paper strips together with glue, or to shorten lines by unsticking or cutting them again.

Pages 14–15: Heavy and light

Fill a balloon with a little water and blow it up, then blow up an empty balloon. Ask children to compare the weight of each balloon. What do the balloons look like? What do they feel like? Why do they feel different? Children may also enjoy wrapping parcels and trying to guess which is lightest/heaviest. Explain to children why size isn't always an indication of weight.

Pages 16–17: Circus time

Introduce children to a range of circus activities such as juggling, spinning a hula hoop or balancing on a narrow beam. Encourage children to count during these activities to test their skills over a period of time. Using a sand timer could set them a challenge!

Pages 18–19: Fill it up!

Help children to explore the volume of liquids and solids by pouring sand or water from one container to another. Which containers hold more sand or water? Which containers hold less? Children may also enjoy making their own rain gauge to measure rainfall, or making a bag or basket (from card or material) to carry small items.

Pages 20–21: Hot and cold

Ask children to sort through a dressing-up box to choose clothes that are good to wear when it's hot or cold. Talk to children about Sun safety, and encourage them to think about how temperature can affect the weather. Why does it snow in winter? Why does it feel hot in summer?

Index

b
big **10, 11**

c
cold **20, 21**

f
far **6, 8**
fill **18, 19**

h
heavy **14, 15**
hot **20**

l
light **14**
long **5, 6, 7**

m
measure **4, 5, 6, 9, 10**

n
near **9**

s
scales **15**
short **5, 7**
small **10**

t
tall **4**
temperature **20, 21**
thick **12**
thin **12, 13**
time **16, 17**

v
volume **18, 19**

w
weight **14, 15**

Picture acknowledgements:
CG textures: cover table; **Corbis:** 4 (Randy Faris), 5 (ultra.f), 10 (Andersen Ross/Blend Images), 16; **Dreamstime:** 6 (Anke Van Wyk), 13 (Redbaron); **Getty Images:** 8 (Mike Harrington), 11 (Jade Albert Studio, Inc.), 18 (Judith Haeusler), 20 (Sun Star), 21 (Andre Gallant); **IStockphoto:** cover sky, 2-3 grass (JLF Capture), 7 (Konstantin Yemel), 12 (Nigel Silcock), 14 (Susan Daniels), 17 (Miroslava Arnaudova), 22-23 grass (JLF Capture), 24 grass (JLF Capture); **Photolibrary:** cover, 15 (Ken Karp), 9 (Willy de l'Horme), 19 (Evan Sklar).